OBAMA'S 36

NEW &

HIGHER

TAXES

HITTING EVERY
INCOME LEVEL

GLEN W. PARK, J. D.

GLEN W. PARK

OBAMA'S 36 NEW & HIGHER TAXES
HITTING EVERY INCOME LEVEL

Transasset, Inc.
Publications Division
P. O. Box 17181
Salt Lake City, UT 84117

ISBN: 978-1479365609

ISBN-10: 1479365602

Library of Congress Control Number. Applied for

Cover Design by Anne P. Inouye

Cover Image licensed from Dreamstime. Used by Permission

Printed in the United States of America

10 9 8 7 6 5 4 3 2 1

CONTENTS

INTRODUCTION

WHY I WROTE THIS BOOK

Throughout the 2012 presidential campaign, very little has been said about one matter that has heretofore always been a major campaign issue—higher taxes. The individual mandate in obamacare is about the only tax about which anyone has talked. Reference to even that new tax died down a short time after the United States Supreme Court's ridiculous decision on obamacare.

The fact is, there are at least 36 new and higher taxes for which Obama and his Democratic minions in Congress are solely responsible!

My purpose in writing this book is to expose Obama's socialist agenda of income redistribution, documenting each new tax, plus the new and onerous regulations associated with those 36 new and higher taxes. I also discuss the horrible consequences to the U. S. economy and to taxpayers in **every** income tax bracket. The one who bears responsibility is Barack Obama, the enemy of America's free enterprise system. It is Obama who is fighting to cripple our capitalist system—the greatest and most prosperous economic system the world has ever known.

This free enterprise system grants its citizens the liberty to reap the benefits of education, hard work, innovation and risk-taking. Because it has not tried to control private enterprise, it has far surpassed every other economic system this world has ever known. If fact, in only 100 years, our economy came to create 50% of the wealth that was being produced in the entire world!

Today, Obama and his congressional cronies threaten to "transform' this great country into a second rate socialist one.

CHAPTER 1

OBAMA WANTS MORE TAXES AND REGULATIONS, BUT AMERICA NEEDS LOWER TAXES AND LESS GOVERNMENT INTERFERENCE

". . . theoretically there is nothing that can stop the government from taxing 100 percent of income so long as the people get benefits from the government commensurate with their income which is taxed." —Barack H. Obama, Sr.

"Whenever he talks about taxing the richest two percent, I think even though he knows that will harm the economy — to him, that redistribution of wealth is still extremely important." — Dr. John C. Drew

"I contend that for a nation to try to tax itself into prosperity is like a man standing in a bucket and trying to lift himself up by the handle." —Sir Winston Churchill

"A government which robs Peter to pay Paul can always depend on the support of Paul." —George Bernard Shaw

On June 29, 2012, the U. S. Supreme Court announced its flawed and pathetic decision upholding most of obamacare, Obama's health care monstrosity. The central issue in the case brought by 26 states' attorneys general was the individual mandate. That provision requires that all Americans have health insurance.

Effective in 2014, those who do not will be penalized with a fee to be collected by the Internal Revenue Service.

All during the process of campaigning for and passing that legislation, euphemistically named "Patient Protection and Affordable Care Act," Obama and the Democrats in the House and Senate promised everyone that this individual mandate was not a tax. They did not want to admit they were raising anyone's taxes.

The Supreme Court, although wrong in its 5 to 4 majority opinion upholding most of obamacare, was correct in stating that this mandate is a tax. Obama still cannot bring himself to admit that obvious fact. But my primary focus in this book is not just that individual mandate. What is astounding to me is that everyone is myopically focused on obamacare's individual mandate being or not being a tax.

The fact is, there are at least 36 new and higher taxes already in place to hammer the American people and our fragile economy—thanks to Obama and his Democratic minions in Congress! The individual mandate is only one of them and is certainly not the biggest or worst of the new taxes.

Yes, horrendously excessive tax increases are already the law because of legislation already passed by Obama and his Democratic cronies in the 2009-2010 Congress. Some have already hit, but most are yet to strike. Obviously, Obama and the Democrats do not want to have everyone be aware of the number and magnitude of the 36 new and higher taxes that are soon to strike. Together, these 36 will constitute the largest increase in taxes in the history of our country. Furthermore, you can be certain that if Americans make the colossal blunder of reelecting Obama in November 2012, this largest-ever tax increase will be only the start for this tax-oholic socialist.

The overwhelming tax increases will come from the numerous repressive and economy-stifling laws Obama has sought and that his Democratic Congress has already passed. In addition, the Bush-era tax cuts will expire after December 31, 2012. They would have already ended on December 31, 2010. But because the Democrats received such a beating in the November 2010 mid-term elections, Obama agreed to extend those tax cuts for two years. Undoubtedly, he hoped American voters would reelect him and he would let those tax cuts expire forever. Therefore, they are again set to expire after midnight, December 31, 2012.

Obama supporters will argue that he has proposed to extend those cuts, but only for those couples making less than $250,000. They carefully avoid noting that his proposed extension is for only one year. Then, all low- and middle-income families will automatically be hit with even those significant tax increases.

The only reason the Bush-era tax cuts were not made permanent in the first place is that in the Senate back in 2001 and 2003, when the tax cuts were being debated, Democrats refused to let those bills come up for a vote under normal procedures. Through the process called "reconciliation," which deals with budget resolutions, the Republican-controlled Senate needed only fifty-one votes to pass those tax cuts. The reasoning was that the budget resolution involved revenue issues, including tax cuts. Any bill passed using reconciliation can only last ten years. Thus, those cuts had an original expiration date of December 31, 2010. Can you believe that Democrats wouldn't want tax cuts to be permanent? Because the tax cuts were already set to automatically expire, the future tax increases would occur without Democrats having to later vote for the tax increases. It is easy to believe that tax- and spend-happy Democrats would fight for such a result.

Remember, President Obama promised in 2008 that if he was elected, there would be absolutely no tax increases for families making less than $250,000 per year. But in order to cover his lie—at least somewhat—Obama thereafter changed his rhetoric, ever so slightly. His words morphed into: he won't be raising "income" taxes on families. But as usual, the reality is far different from what Obama says. Reality is even far different from his "revised" promise. We will see just how great that difference is.

Congress, before their 2010 election break, voted not to deal with an extension of the Bush-era tax cuts that Republicans in Congress had pushed for. Even a so-called "blue dog Democrat" from a Republican state had publicly campaigned, saying, "To raise taxes now for anyone in this economy would be a mistake." He was only following the usual Democrat line—say what sounds good to constituents—then do the opposite. He cast the deciding vote in lock-step with his radical Democratic colleagues. The result was to adjourn Congress prior to the 2010 election break, rather than even consider extending those tax cuts. Voting to consider extension and then to extend those tax cuts would have let the business community—those who create real jobs—know that they could expect reasonable continuity in the coming year. Extending them for everyone would have actually helped prevent further job losses in small and large companies alike. But it would have helped more if the extension had been passed early in 2010, or even before that. But to do that, Obama and Democrats would have needed intelligence, concern for American jobs, plus the moral courage to do so. No company in 2010 wanted to hire new employees, knowing that taxes were to soon increase, and even thereafter, continue to climb.

But Republicans won a large majority of the 2010 congressional races and took back seven Senate seats. Because of those substantial wins, Obama was put in a position he had not yet experienced—Congress would no longer walk in lock-step with his foolish, anti-American policies.

It is documented history that Obama and congressional Democrats originally refused to even consider extending the Bush-era tax cuts set to expire on December 31, 2010. Then they were taken to the woodshed and given an old-fashioned beating—or as Obama, in one of his few honest statements correctly labeled it—"a shellacking"—in the November 2010 election. Then, all of a sudden, Obama caved, and the congressional Democrats were dragged, kicking and screaming, to continue the tax cuts for "the rich." Of course, Obama had set his own concocted definition of "the rich" as those couples earning more than $250,000 annually. Obama set another day of reckoning—December 31, 2012—when the current extension will end. Hopefully, Democrats' numbers will be further decimated in November 2012. And hopefully, our country will have a different President—one who loves America, wants to help its economy, wants liberty and prosperity for its citizens and understands how to do all of that. Obama doesn't.

Let's consider how Obama and other Democrats view tax cuts, or even maintaining current tax rates for so-called "rich" Americans. Vice President Joe Biden moaned that although it was necessary, and even beneficial for the U. S. economy to have the Bush-era tax cuts extended, it was "morally repugnant" to him. It was morally repugnant to the Democrats, although they admit it was necessary and even beneficial for the U. S. economy! Amazing.

Such blind greed from Biden, Obama and the other Democrats is repugnant to me and to most reasonable-thinking, freedom-loving Americans.

After the huge 2010 election losses, Republicans were in a position where Obama could not just dictate and turn his back on the Republicans. They no longer had to "sit at the back of the bus." Obama could no longer get his wants from a Democrat near-super majority in Congress. Obama had to actually listen to and deal with the Republicans.

You may remember that just before the November 2010 election, Obama criticized Republicans, telling them that they could essentially "come along," but they would have to go to the back of the bus. His exact words were:

> Now that progress has been made, we can't have special interests sitting shotgun. We gotta have middle class families up in front. We don't mind the Republicans joining us. They can come for the ride, but they gotta sit in back.[1]

After November 2010, no longer could Obama so arrogantly make such an absurd and ridiculous demand.

One of Obama's specialties—tax increases—will indeed not cease to be his priority after the temporary extension of the Bush-era tax cuts ends. With Obama and most congressional Democrats still wanting to empty our wallets, many more taxes will follow unless Republicans stand firm against them and actually do what is right for our country, its economy and its citizens.

Why does Obama focus so myopically on higher taxes on "the rich?" In an article in *American Thinker*, Paul Kengor recounts his interview with Dr. John C. Drew, Ph.D. Drew met Obama at Occidental College in 1980. Speaking of Obama, Drew said,

> **I can definitely [say] that he [Obama] had a very consistent ideology, . . . I think his current behavior demonstrates that he does still have these ideological convictions. Whenever he talks about taxing the richest two percent, I think even though he knows that will harm the economy—to him, that redistribution of wealth is still extremely important. And I think the problem here is that . . . [h]e never had any real business experience, never had a payroll to meet, and I think he still is locked in a very dangerous mindset where I think if he didn't fight to redistribute the wealth, he would feel guilty . . .**[2]
> (emphasis added).

The reason for Obama feeling no hesitancy about raising taxes can be found in his dreams—inherited from his father. Obama, Sr. felt that taxes could not be raised too high. He said:

> **". . . theoretically there is nothing that can stop the government from taxing 100 percent of income so long as the people get benefits from the**

11

government commensurate with their income which is taxed."[3]

Obviously, this is inefficient and evil. First, an enormous government bureaucracy is necessary to run such a Soviet, Marxist government. The Soviet Union had a giant bureaucracy. It also had to have a brutally-repressive secret police to keep its citizens under its repressive control. That bureaucracy's costs came off the top. Second, most of what was left was re-distributed. This is insane to contemplate! But it is part of Obama's inherited dream. We should remember how such a Soviet system stifled individual initiative and innovation. It is hard to believe why Obama is fighting so hard to copy that failed system.

I will now list some of the huge tax increases coming, courtesy of Obama. These will come from four sources: (1) obamacare—which imposes at least twenty-two new taxes; (2) employer tax hikes; (3) the Alternative Minimum Tax; and (4) the approaching end of the once-extended Bush-era tax cuts—which now conveniently expire on December 31, 2012—after the next presidential and congressional elections in November 2012.

Again, at least twenty-two new or higher taxes are written into the crippling obamacare law. Some began in 2010! In addition to obamacare's new taxes, at least 14 new or higher taxes strike on or before January 1, 2013. Additional costs to American taxpayers come from Obama's onerous regulations. These are all from Obama's efforts to suck more and more from American taxpayers. The following list shows 36 new or higher taxes and the date each tax strikes American taxpayers. I identify those imposed by obamacare by adding "(UNDER OBAMACARE)" after each tax, with the page numbers in the actual bill(s) that create these taxes. In some cases, the tax is imposed in the original bill, obamacare (PPACA). Others are created in the "Reconciliation" bill that followed passage of obamacare. I state who will be hurt by each new and higher tax. **Nearly all of them hammer low- and**

middle-income taxpayers, not just higher-income ones. Sometimes, the harm to all taxpayers comes from increased costs passed on to them as consumers. After listing these taxes, we will analyze more closely the damage from each. Read and weep.

THE LIST OF OBAMA'S 36 NEW AND HIGHER TAXES

NEW OBAMA TAX #1 - Individual Mandate Excise Tax (January 2014), (UNDER OBAMACARE), (Pages 317-337). **HAMMERS LOW, MIDDLE AND HIGH INCOME TAXPAYERS.**

NEW OBAMA TAX #2 – The "Employer-Provided Health Insurance Tax" - (2010), (UNDER OBAMACARE), (Page 1,957). **HAMMERS LOW, MIDDLE AND HIGH INCOME TAXPAYERS.**

NEW OBAMA TAX #3 - The "Special-Needs Kids Tax" - (January 2013), (UNDER OBAMACARE), (Pages 2,388-2,389). **HAMMERS LOW, MIDDLE AND HIGH INCOME TAXPAYERS.**

NEW/HIGHER OBAMA TAX #4 – Increase in Medicare Payroll Tax - (January 2013), (UNDER OBAMACARE), (PPACA: Pages 2,000-2,003, and Reconciliation Act: Pages 87-93). **HAMMERS LOW, MIDDLE AND HIGH INCOME TAXPAYERS.**

NEW OBAMA TAX #5 - Employer Mandate Tax (January 2014), (UNDER OBAMACARE), (Pages 345-346). **HAMMERS LOW, MIDDLE AND HIGH INCOME TAXPAYERS.**

NEW/HIGHER OBAMA TAX #6 - Surtax on Investment Income – (January 2013), (UNDER OBAMACARE), (Reconciliation Act: Pages 87-93). **HAMMERS LOW, MIDDLE AND HIGH INCOME TAXPAYERS.**

NEW/HIGHER OBAMA TAX #7 - Increase in Threshold to Itemize Deduction of Medical Expenses (January 2013), (UNDER OBAMACARE), (Pages 1,994-1,995). **HAMMERS LOW, MIDDLE AND HIGH INCOME TAXPAYERS.**

NEW OBAMA TAX #8 - HSA tax benefit eliminated - (January 2011), (UNDER OBAMACARE), (Pages 1,957-1,959). **HAMMERS LOW, MIDDLE AND HIGH INCOME TAXPAYERS.**

NEW OBAMA TAX #9 - FSA tax benefit eliminated - (January 2011), (UNDER OBAMACARE), (Pages 1,957-1,959). **HAMMERS LOW, MIDDLE AND HIGH INCOME TAXPAYERS.**

NEW OBAMA TAX #10 - HRA tax benefit eliminated - (January 2011), (UNDER OBAMACARE), (Pages 1,957-1,959). **HAMMERS LOW, MIDDLE AND HIGH INCOME TAXPAYERS.**

NEW OBAMA TAX #11 - The Health Savings Account Withdrawal Tax Hike - (January 2011), (UNDER OBAMACARE), (Page 1,959). **HAMMERS LOW, MIDDLE AND HIGH INCOME TAXPAYERS.**

NEW OBAMA TAX #12 - Excise Tax on Charitable Hospitals (Immediate—2010), (UNDER OBAMACARE), (Pages 1,961-1,971). **HAMMERS LOW, MIDDLE AND HIGH INCOME TAXPAYERS.**

NEW OBAMA TAX #13 - Tax on Innovator Drug Companies (January 2010), (UNDER OBAMACARE), (Pages 1,971-1,980). **HAMMERS LOW, MIDDLE AND HIGH INCOME TAXPAYERS.**

NEW OBAMA TAX #14 - Blue Cross/Blue Shield Tax Hike (January 2010), (UNDER OBAMACARE), (Page 2,004). **HAMMERS LOW, MIDDLE AND HIGH INCOME TAXPAYERS.**

NEW OBAMA TAX #15 - Tax on Indoor Tanning Services (July 1, 2010), (UNDER OBAMACARE), (Pages 2,397-2,399). **HAMMERS LOW, MIDDLE AND HIGH INCOME TAXPAYERS.**

NEW OBAMA TAX #16 - Codification of the "Economic Substance Doctrine" – (April 1, 2010), (UNDER OBAMACARE), (Reconciliation Act: Pages 108-113). **HAMMERS LOW, MIDDLE AND HIGH INCOME TAXPAYERS.**

NEW OBAMA TAX #17 - "Bio-Fuel Tax" – (April 2010), (UNDER OBAMACARE), (Reconciliation Act: Page 105). **HAMMERS LOW, MIDDLE AND HIGH INCOME TAXPAYERS.**

NEW OBAMA TAX #18 - Elimination of the Tax Deduction for Employer-Provided Retirement Rx Drug Coverage in Coordination With Medicare Part D – (January 2013), (UNDER OBAMACARE), (Page 1,994). **HAMMERS LOW, MIDDLE AND HIGH INCOME TAXPAYERS.**

NEW OBAMA TAX #19 - $500,000 Annual Executive Compensation Limit for Health Insurance Executives – (January 2013), (UNDER OBAMACARE), (Pages 1,995-2,000). **HAMMERS HIGH INCOME TAXPAYERS.**

NEW OBAMA TAX #20 - Tax on Medical Device Manufacturers – (January 2013), (UNDER OBAMACARE), (Pages 1,980-1,986). **HAMMERS LOW, MIDDLE AND HIGH INCOME TAXPAYERS.**

<u>NEW OBAMA TAX #21</u> - Tax on Health Insurers – (January 2014), (UNDER OBAMACARE), (Pages 1,986-1,993), **HAMMERS LOW, MIDDLE AND HIGH INCOME TAXPAYERS.**

<u>NEW OBAMA TAX #22</u> - Excise Tax on Comprehensive Health Insurance Plans – (January 2018), (UNDER OBAMACARE), (Pages 1,941-1,946). **HAMMERS LOW, MIDDLE AND HIGH INCOME TAXPAYERS.**

<u>HIGHER OBAMA TAX #23</u> – Tax Brackets Go Up For Everyone – **TAXPAYERS IN THE LOWEST TAX BRACKET WILL HAVE THEIR TAX RATES INCREASE BY 50%! HAMMERS LOW, MIDDLE AND HIGH INCOME TAXPAYERS.**

<u>HIGHER OBAMA TAX #24</u> - The child tax credit will be cut in half, from $1,000 to $500 per child. **HAMMERS LOW, MIDDLE AND HIGH INCOME TAXPAYERS.**

<u>HIGHER OBAMA TAX #25</u> - The dependent care tax credit will be cut. **HAMMERS LOW, MIDDLE AND HIGH INCOME TAXPAYERS.**

<u>HIGHER OBAMA TAX #26</u> - The adoption tax credit will be cut. **HAMMERS LOW, MIDDLE AND HIGH INCOME TAXPAYERS.**

<u>HIGHER OBAMA TAX #27</u> - Return of the Death Tax. **HAMMERS LOW, MIDDLE AND HIGH INCOME TAXPAYERS.**

<u>HIGHER OBAMA TAX #28</u> - There will be higher taxes on marriage. **HAMMERS LOW, MIDDLE AND HIGH INCOME TAXPAYERS.**

HIGHER OBAMA TAX #29 - The capital gains tax will rise from 15% in 2010 through 2012 to 23.8% in 2013. **HAMMERS LOW, MIDDLE AND HIGH INCOME TAXPAYERS.**

HIGHER OBAMA TAX #30 - The tax on dividends will rise to 39.6% in 2013! **HAMMERS MIDDLE AND HIGH INCOME TAXPAYERS.**

HIGHER OBAMA TAX #31 – Leaving Un-Indexed The Alternative Minimum Tax. **HAMMERS LOW, MIDDLE AND HIGH INCOME TAXPAYERS.**

HIGHER OBAMA TAX #32 - Charitable Contributions from IRAs will no longer be allowed – (January 2013). **HAMMERS LOW, MIDDLE AND HIGH INCOME TAXPAYERS.**

HIGHER OBAMA TAX #33 - Reduction of Tax Deductions for Education and Teaching – (January 2013). **HAMMERS LOW, MIDDLE AND HIGH INCOME TAXPAYERS.**

HIGHER OBAMA TAX #34 –Less write-off of equipment purchases. (January 2013). **HAMMERS LOW, MIDDLE AND HIGH INCOME TAXPAYERS.**

HIGHER OBAMA TAX #35 - 50% expensing will disappear. (January 2013). **HAMMERS LOW, MIDDLE AND HIGH INCOME TAXPAYERS.**

HIGHER OBAMA TAX #36 – (January 2012) Tax credit for research and experimentation has already expired. **HAMMERS LOW, MIDDLE AND HIGH INCOME TAXPAYERS.**

.

CHAPTER 2

ANALYSIS OF OBAMA'S 36 NEW TAXES

NEW OBAMA TAX #1 - **Individual Mandate Excise Tax (January 2014), (UNDER OBAMACARE)**, (Pages 317-337): Anyone not buying qualifying health insurance must pay an income surtax according to the higher of the following:

Year	For 1 Adult	For 2 Adults	For 3+ Adults
2014	1% AGI or $95	1% AGI or $190	1% AGI or $285
2014	2% AGI or $325	2% AGI or $650	2% AGI or $975
2016	2.5% AGI or $695	2.5% AGI or $1,390	2.5% AGI or $2,085

NOTE: **There are exemptions for undocumented immigrants, prisoners**, religious objectors, those earning less than the federal poverty line, members of Indian tribes and hardship cases—as may be determined by Health and Human Services (HHS)! **This will hurt people at all income levels.**

NEW OBAMA TAX #2 – **The "Employer-Provided Health Insurance Tax" - (2010), (UNDER OBAMACARE)**, (Page 1,957): Obama and the Democratic leaders who pushed through the bill have created a tax on insurance premiums your employer pays for you. The W-2 you receive is required to report the value of whatever health insurance your employer provides, whether the employer is a private or governmental entity. It does not matter if you are retired, or if you earn less than Obama's favorite number, $250,000. The premiums paid are added to your gross income.

You are now required to pay taxes on a large sum of money that you have never actually seen. However much your employer-paid insurance premiums are, your income on which your taxes will be calculated will increase by that same amount. Plus, often that much extra income could put you in a higher tax bracket. That means (1) you will pay more in taxes for your employer-provided premiums; and (2) you may pay taxes at a higher income tax rate.

Anyone may argue that point, but I reviewed the tax return of a retired man and his working wife who received $3,200 in health insurance premiums from an employer. This couple, making under $60,000 in income, saw their federal income tax increase by $892 and their state income tax increase by $377, for a total of $1,269 in additional taxes! So much for Obama's promise that if he was elected, no couple making under $250,000 would pay more in taxes! Likewise, so much for his later modified promise that there would be no such increase in "income taxes." How much should one conclude his promises are worth? For that couple alone, a negative $1,269. **This tax will hurt people at all income levels.**

NEW OBAMA TAX #3 - **The "Special-Needs Kids Tax" - (January 2013)**, **(UNDER OBAMACARE)**, **(**Pages 2,388-2,389): Obamacare imposes a cap on flexible spending accounts (FSAs) of $2,500. Before obamacare struck in this area, there was no federal government limit. There are thousands of families with special needs children in the United States that use FSAs to pay for special needs education who will be hit hard. Tuition rates at special needs schools can range up to more than $14,000 per year. Under obamacare, FSA dollars cannot be used to pay for this type of special needs education! Isn't it nice to know how much Obama and other Democrats really care about those with special needs? What about their claims that they are looking out for the "little" guy or the disadvantaged? **This tax will hurt all income levels.**

NEW/HIGHER OBAMA TAX #4 – Increase in Medicare Payroll Tax - (January 2013), (UNDER OBAMACARE), (PPACA: Page 2,000-2,003, and Reconciliation Act: Page 87-93): Employees currently have 1.45% of their wages deducted for the Medicare payroll tax. Effective January 1, 2013, workers will lose 2.35% to the Medicare payroll tax. **That is a 62% increase!** **This will hurt people at all income levels.**

NEW OBAMA TAX #5 - Employer Mandate Tax (January 2014), (UNDER OBAMACARE), (Pages 345-346): If an employer with 50 or more employees does not offer health coverage, and at least one employee qualifies for a health tax credit, the employer must pay an additional non-deductible tax of $2,000 for all full-time employees. That's $2,000 times 50+! If any employee actually receives coverage through an exchange set up under obamacare, the penalty on the employer for that employee increases to $3,000. If the employer requires a waiting period to enroll in coverage of 30-60 days, there is a penalty of $400 tax per employee ($600 if the waiting period is 60 days or longer). **This will hurt people at all income levels.**

NEW/HIGHER OBAMA TAX #6 - Surtax on Investment Income – (January 2013), (UNDER OBAMACARE), (Reconciliation Act: Pages 87-93): This involves the creation of a new, 3.8% surtax on investment income earned in households making at least $200,000 ($250,000 if married.) This tax was a last-minute addition to the Reconciliation Act of 2010 and was never introduced, discussed or reviewed until just hours before the final debate on the massive health care legislation began. NOTE: **This 3.8% surtax does NOT apply to non-resident aliens!**

NEW/HIGHER OBAMA TAX #7 - Increase in Threshold to Itemize Deduction of Medical Expenses (January 2013), (UNDER OBAMACARE), (Page 1,994-1,995): Currently, we can itemize for deduction any medical expenses exceeding 7.5% of adjusted gross income (AGI). The threshold for such itemizations will increase to 10%, thereby reducing the portion of high medical expenses that can be deducted from taxable income. For 2013-2016 only, this increase is waived for taxpayers 65 and older. Thereafter, they will also face the increased threshold. **This will hurt people at all income levels.**

The "Medical Savings Taxes" (UNDER OBAMACARE):

NEW OBAMA TAX #8 - HSA tax benefit eliminated - (January 2011), (UNDER OBAMACARE), (Pages 1,957-1,959): Americans will no longer be able to use **health savings account** (HSA) pre-tax dollars to purchase non-prescription, over-the-counter medicines (except insulin). **This will hurt people at all income levels.**

NEW OBAMA TAX #9 - FSA tax benefit eliminated - (January 2011), (UNDER OBAMACARE), (Pages 1,957-1,959): Americans will no longer be able to use **flexible spending account** (FSA) pre-tax dollars to purchase non-prescription, over-the-counter medicines (except insulin). **This will hurt all income levels.**

NEW OBAMA TAX #10 - HRA tax benefit eliminated - (January 2011), (UNDER OBAMACARE), (Pages 1957-1959): Americans will no longer be able to use **health reimbursement account** (HRA) pre-tax dollars to purchase non-prescription, over-the-counter medicines (except insulin). **This will hurt people at all income levels.**

NEW OBAMA TAX #11 - The Health Savings Account Withdrawal Tax Hike - (January 2011), (UNDER OBAMACARE), (Page 1,959): Obamacare increases the additional tax on non-medical early withdrawals from a health savings account (HSA) from 10% to 20%. **This will hurt people at all income levels.**

NEW OBAMA TAX #12 - **Excise Tax on Charitable Hospitals (Immediate—2010), (UNDER OBAMACARE),** (Pages 1,961-1,971): $50,000 per hospital if it fails to meet new "community health assessment needs," "financial assistance," and billing and collection" rules set by the Department of Health and Human Services (HHS). **This will hurt people at all income levels.**

NEW OBAMA TAX #13 - **Tax on Innovator Drug Companies (January 2010), (UNDER OBAMACARE),** (Pages 1,971-1,980): $2.3 billion annual tax on the industry imposed relative to the share of sales made that year. **So Obama wants to discourage new and innovative medicines from being invented. This shows another way in which obamacare is NOT health care reform. It is a health care destroyer. This will hurt people at all income levels.**

NEW OBAMA TAX #14 - **Blue Cross/Blue Shield Tax Hike (January 2010), (UNDER OBAMACARE),** (Page 2,004): Special tax deduction in current law for Blue Cross/Blue Shield companies is allowed only if 85% or more of premium revenues are spent on clinical services. **This will hurt people at all income levels.**

NEW OBAMA TAX #15 - **Tax on Indoor Tanning Services (July 1, 2010), (UNDER OBAMACARE),** (Pages 2,397-2,399): Customers will pay a 10% tax on the price of tanning services. **This will hurt people at all income levels.**

NEW OBAMA TAX #16 - **Codification of the "Economic Substance Doctrine" – (April 1, 2010), (UNDER OBAMACARE)**, (Reconciliation Act: Pages 108-113): This provision allows the IRS to disallow otherwise entirely legal tax deductions and other legal tax-minimizing plans just because the IRS deems that the action lacks "substance" and is merely intended to reduce taxes owed. This codification can result in a penalty of up to 40% of the tax not paid for any transactions deemed by the Internal Revenue Service to "lack economic substance". **This will hurt people at all income levels.**

NEW OBAMA TAX #17 - **"Bio-Fuel Tax" – (April 2010), (UNDER OBAMACARE)**, (Reconciliation Act: Page 105): This increases the tax on a type of bio-fuel, which will increase its cost to consumers. **This will hurt people at all income levels.**

NEW OBAMA TAX #18 - **Elimination of the Tax Deduction for Employer-Provided Retirement Rx Drug Coverage in Coordination With Medicare Part D (January 2013), (UNDER OBAMACARE)**, (Page 1,994): This will encourage employers to drop such retirement prescription drug coverage for their employees. **This will hurt people at all income levels.**

NEW OBAMA TAX #19 - **$500,000 Annual Executive Compensation Limit for Health Insurance Executives (January 2013), (UNDER OBAMACARE)**, (Pages 1,995-2,000): Obama and Democrats obviously believe they have the right to dictate how much people should earn. Dictators in all countries, including the former Soviet Union, have always had this same arrogant belief. **This will hurt people in upper income levels.**

NEW OBAMA TAX #20 - **Tax on Medical Device Manufacturers (January 2013), (UNDER OBAMACARE)**, (Pages 1,980-1,986): Medical device manufacturers employ 360,000 people in 6,000 plants across the U. S. Obamacare imposes a new 2.3% excise tax on the devices they manufacture that retail over $100. This will certainly NOT help to reduce health care costs! It will increase them. **This will hurt people at all income levels.**

NEW OBAMA TAX #21 - **Tax on Health Insurers (January 2014), (UNDER OBAMACARE)**, (Pages 1,986-1,993): This annual tax on the health insurance industry is imposed according to the health insurance premiums collected in any given year. The tax phases in until 2018, when it is fully imposed on companies with $50 million or more in profits. This can only increase insurance premiums. **This will hurt people at all income levels.**

NEW OBAMA TAX #22 - **Excise Tax on Comprehensive Health Insurance Plans (January 2018), (UNDER OBAMACARE)**, (Pages 1,941-1,946): There will be a new 40% excise tax on so-called "Cadillac" health insurance plans ($10,200 per single/$27,500 per family annual premiums paid). For high-risk professions and early retirees, there is a higher threshold ($11,500 per single and $29,450 per family). This is CPI + 1 percentage point indexed.[4], [5], [6] **This will hurt people at all income levels.**

FOURTEEN ADDITIONAL HIGHER TAXES
December 31, 2012 expiration of the temporarily-extended Bush-era tax cuts: As mentioned earlier, on January 1, 2013, the day following the end of this temporary extension, taxes will increase dramatically in the following areas:

HIGHER OBAMA TAX #23 - **Tax Brackets Go Up For Everyone. TAXPAYERS IN THE LOWEST TAX BRACKET WILL HAVE THEIR TAX RATES INCREASE BY 50%!: Personal income tax rates will rise for everyone.**

From the lowest to the highest rate, every taxpayer's taxes will go up. To illustrate, I will simply list the expiring rates and the coming new rates. **This will hurt people at all income levels.**

Expiring Brackets		Brackets to come
10%	- will increase to -	15%
25%	- will increase to -	28%
28%	- will increase to -	31%
33%	- will increase to -	36%
35%	- will increase to -	39.6%

There will be higher taxes on families as follows:

<u>**HIGHER OBAMA TAX #24**</u> - **The child tax credit will be cut in half**, from $1,000 to $500 per child. **This will hurt people at all income levels.**

<u>**HIGHER OBAMA TAX #25**</u> - **The dependent care tax credit will be cut. This will hurt people at all income levels.**

<u>**HIGHER OBAMA TAX #26**</u> - **The adoption tax credit will be cut. This will hurt people at all income levels.**

<u>**HIGHER OBAMA TAX #27**</u> - **Return of the Death Tax**: As stated herein above, in 2010, there was no death tax. For those who die on or after January 1, 2011 until December 31, 2012, there is a 35% death tax rate on estates over $5 million! If this is allowed to expire, beginning on January 1, 2013 it will become a whopping 55% on estates over $1 million! A person leaving behind two homes and a retirement account could easily pass along a whopping death tax to his surviving loved ones who may be required to dispose of one or both of the homes in a fire-sale way just to pay

the enormous tax! Doing so will not leave much of the estate for which the decedent worked his whole life to provide for the loved ones he left behind. In addition to working all of his life to so provide, he also already paid taxes on the income used to build such a nest egg. But the Democrats in the White House and Congress believe they are more entitled to that nest egg than his children. So Obama and the Democrats are fully willing—no, thrilled—to double tax it. **This will hurt people at all income levels.**

HIGHER OBAMA TAX #28 - **There will be higher taxes on marriage**: The "marriage penalty", which is created by narrower (higher) tax brackets for married couples, will return from the very first dollar of income on up. Plus, the standard deduction will no longer be doubled for married couples, relative to the single-person level. **This will hurt married people at all income levels.**

Higher Tax Rates for Savers and Investors:

HIGHER OBAMA TAX #29 - **The capital gains tax will rise** from 15% in 2010 through 2012 to 23.8% in 2013. **This will hurt people at all income levels.**

HIGHER OBAMA TAX #30 - **The tax on dividends will rise** to 39.6% in 2013! This will only discourage investment in companies that provide jobs for American workers.

HIGHER OBAMA TAX #31 - **The Alternative Minimum Tax (AMT)**: When Americans filed their tax returns for 2010, many (up to 28.5 million families) confronted a cruel addition to their taxes. Since our wonderful 2009-2010 Democrat-controlled Congress refused to index the AMT, with Obama's strong support, this alternative minimum tax will hurt a significant percentage of taxpayers by hitting them with a far-higher tax.

Note: The alternative minimum tax (AMT) was instituted in 1969 to catch a very small number of taxpayers with significant income who otherwise could use various deductions to keep from paying any tax.

Because of inflation—mostly caused by our federal government's inability to control its spending—nearly everyone's income has gone up virtually every year. That may not mean that a given person with a higher dollar amount earned can actually buy any more. Generally, as wages and other income increase, so does the cost of everything a person buys. So in reality, his real, inflation-adjusted income remains constant and sometimes even declines. But because the non-indexed dollar amount gets higher, the person can move into a higher tax bracket. This means his taxes increase, even though his real buying power has remained the same or actually declined. Additionally, as income increases, the AMT excludes deductions that could have been used to reduce income taxes, thereby further increasing income taxes. So there continue to be two stings for the price of the short-sightedness and greed of Obama and the Democrats in Congress. **This will hurt middle and higher income levels.**

HIGHER OBAMA TAX #32 - Charitable Contributions from IRAs will no longer be allowed – (January 2012): In 2010, a retired person with an Individual Retirement Account (IRA) could contribute up to $100,000 per year directly to a charity from his or her IRA. This contribution would also count toward an annual "required minimum distribution." Beginning in 2011, this ability to contribute directly and count the contribution toward the required minimum distribution ceased. **This will hurt middle and higher income levels.**

HIGHER OBAMA TAX #33 - Reduction of Tax Deductions for Education and Teaching – (January 2013): The deduction for tuition and fees will cease to be available. Tax credits for education will be limited. Teachers will no longer be able to deduct classroom expenses. The student loan interest deduction will be disallowed for hundreds of thousands of families. There will be a cut in Coverdell Education Savings Accounts. The allowance for non-taxable employer-provided educational assistance is reduced. **This will hurt people at all income levels.**

Higher Business Taxes:

HIGHER OBAMA TAX #34 - **Less write-off of equipment purchases**: The ability of small businesses to expense, or write off, certain capital expenditures, instead of depreciating them slowly over a period of years, will be slashed. Businesses have been able to write off equipment purchases up to $250,000 per year. The amount that small businesses will be able to deduct for such purchases from current income will be cut to only $25,000! That could result in far higher federal taxes for those businesses, even small businesses and small business owners. The increase in taxes could be up to nearly $90,000.00 in a single year! **This will hurt people at all income levels.**

HIGHER OBAMA TAX #35 - **50% expensing will disappear**: Fifty percent expensing will totally disappear for larger businesses. Through 2010, larger businesses could expense half (50%) of their equipment purchases. As of January, 2011, one hundred percent (100%) of the equipment purchases of larger businesses must be depreciated. So their federal income taxes will likewise skyrocket! Through price increases passed on to customers, **this will hurt people at all income levels.**

HIGHER OBAMA TAX #36 – **(January 2012) Tax credit for research and experimentation has ended (expired)**: The research and experimentation tax credit is already lost to businesses. This, and the many other tax increases on businesses, will have a net effect of discouraging employers from hiring workers. Employers may even lay off some. This obviously means a loss of jobs. That is just what our country needs with short-sighted obamacare, financial regulation, and other restrictive laws that will continue to cripple the United States, thanks to guess who? This credit was first created in 1981, during the Ronald Reagan administration. Obama and congressional Democrats allowed this credit to expire at the end of 2011. How shortsighted.

Two of the primary things that have made America the most prosperous nation on earth have been: (1) the greatest innovative minds; (2) the liberty to profit from one's innovation and risk. The loss of this tax credit and the other tax increases will stifle both of these. Through the years, the research tax credit has greatly encouraged innovation. Through price increases, **this will hurt people at all income levels.**

CHAPTER 3

OBAMA'S ONEROUS PENALTIES AND REGULATIONS

In addition to the above 36 destructive new and higher taxes Obama has imposed upon Americans, there are onerous penalties and regulations with which Obama will require businesses—small and large alike—to comply. Their cost will seriously harm businesses and increase the cost of their products and services to the American people. They include:

OBAMA'S ONEROUS PENALTY #1 – **Corporate 1099-MISC Information Reporting (January 2012)**, **(UNDER OBAMACARE)**: Requires businesses to send 1099-MISC information tax forms to corporations (previously exempted). This is a huge compliance burden and cost for small employers. **HAMMERS LOW, MIDDLE AND HIGH INCOME TAXPAYERS.**

OBAMA'S ONEROUS PENALTY #2 - **Higher costs to employers for new hires (UNDER OBAMACARE)**: There is a penalty on employers who hire low-income employees. Employers will be required to pay for insurance in behalf of these newly-hired employees. This is a huge disincentive for employers to hire. Therefore, it is not an incentive that will help produce additional jobs in our economy that needs new jobs so badly. **HAMMERS LOW, MIDDLE AND HIGH INCOME TAXPAYERS.**

OBAMA'S ONEROUS PENALTY #3 - **Higher costs to Medicare and Medicaid recipients** - **(UNDER**

OBAMACARE): Medicare and Medicaid recipients—especially women—will have less of their care paid for. Thus, they will receive worse care but will be required to pay by themselves for a higher portion of that inferior care. **HAMMERS LOW, MIDDLE AND HIGH INCOME TAXPAYERS.**

OBAMA'S EXCESSIVE REGULATION #4 - **Dramatically increased costs and restrictions of new regulations still to come - (UNDER OBAMACARE)**: There will be many additional regulations promulgated under obamacare that will significantly increase costs—the same result as additional taxes—to individuals and companies. **HAMMERS LOW, MIDDLE AND HIGH INCOME TAXPAYERS.**

President Ronald Reagan told us exactly how government is. This is especially the case if Obama and other Democrats get to determine much about it. He said:

Government's view of the economy could be summed up in a few short phrases: If it moves, tax it. If it keeps moving, regulate it. And if it stops moving, subsidize it.[7]

He knew what he was talking about. He worked for eight years as Governor of California with a Democrat-dominated legislature, and then for eight years as President, battling a Democrat-dominated House of Representatives.

Obama's and Congress' constant desire to take more from taxpayers brings to mind a prescient and truthful statement made by that great American founder and statesman, Benjamin Franklin. He must have seen Obama and today's Democrats as he correctly stated: **"When the people find that they can vote themselves money, that will herald the end of the republic."**[8]

Obama and his cronies have moved well beyond the discovery. They have made it an art form. It is their mode of operation in everything they do. They are creating more and more "Pauls" who are dependent upon a big-brother government.

NOTE: There is something we citizens can do about these coming tax increases. We can vote out of office the chief impediments to their revocation—Obama and every Democrat on the ballot in November 2012 for the House and Senate! If Obama and a vast majority of Democrats in the House and Senate are re-elected, then say "Hello" and "Yes sir" to all kinds of increased taxes and onerous regulations, while you say "Goodbye" to the potential of real economic growth, job creation and keeping most of the money you earn.

Unless one is willing to ignore the obvious truth, it is absolutely easy to know who is responsible for the anti-business direction our country is currently taking. They are: Obama and the other intentionally malignant Democrats in the White House, Senate and House who are 100% responsible for these new and higher taxes and the related onerous regulations. Remember, not one Republican voted for obamacare. And Democrats absolutely do not want to maintain the economy-assisting Bush-era tax cuts. To summarize, whether because of malignantly evil and intentional actions or sheer incompetence, the disastrous results are the same. Innocent people and our country are seriously harmed. Taxpayers in every income tax bracket will continue to be hammered. We are fast approaching the tax-increase cliff.

CHAPTER 4

DISASTROUS CONSEQUENCES OF OBAMA'S NEW TAXES

A new study by Ernst & Young concludes: Increasing taxes on higher-income Americans will result in higher taxes for 2.1 Million business owners, reduce economic output by $200 Billion and <u>cost 710,000 jobs</u>!

Obama's new and higher taxes on the so-called "rich" will result in only enough additional tax revenue to operate his profligate government for about eight (8) days!

Obama has consistently claimed that his focus has been on creating jobs. The fact is that his policies have prevented hundreds of thousands, even millions, of jobs from being created. He and his Democratic minions seem incapable of understanding—or maybe they just don't care—that higher taxes and more overreaching regulations keep businesses from expanding. Plus, Obama and the Democrats just don't "get it"—that uncertainty over new taxes does the same thing. The result, which should not surprise anyone with even mediocre intelligence, is that fewer jobs will be created.

In our struggling economy in which unemployment has exceeded eight percent for 43 consecutive months (as of September 2012), Obama continues to preach raising taxes on his so-called "rich." The national accounting firm, Ernst & Young, recently released the findings of its study concerning Obama's insistence on raising those taxes. Their conclusion: **Increasing taxes on higher-income Americans will result in higher taxes for 2.1**

million business owners, reduce economic output by $200 billion and cost 710,000 jobs.[9] So much for Obama's bogus claims that his constant focus is on creating jobs.

The disaster gets even worse. Ernst & Young also declared that 900,000 business owners will see their taxes increase. That will result in horrible consequences for taxpayers at all income levels: low-, middle- and high-income taxpayers! Businesses will lay off employees. Many businesses will hire fewer new workers. Plus, businesses will pass on their increased costs to customers. That will further dampen consumer spending, the result of which will be additional lay-offs and decreased new hiring.

The net result of Obama's wrong-headed push for higher taxes on his so-called "rich" will cost jobs and hurt, not help, the economy.

The disastrous consequences do not end there. Obama's new and higher taxes under obamacare will increase taxes on all income levels—even low-income taxpayers.

The majority of the tax increases will hit baby boomers. Their average tax increase will be $4,200 per year. Low-income taxpayers will see their taxes increase by $1,200 per year. Millenials' taxes will go up by $1,000 per year. Everyone will see increased costs of products and services.

Let's add up the consequences of Obama's wrong-headed, socialist desire to raise taxes. (1) Already we have nearly four years of unemployment over eight percent. (2) Obama's new and higher taxes will result in 710,000 additional jobs lost. (3) Consumer spending will necessarily decline. (4) Consumers will pay higher prices. (5) Low-income taxpayers, baby boomers and millenials will all be hit with higher taxes.

All of those harmful economic consequences come to the majority of taxpayers for what benefit? Obama's new and higher taxes (and negative economic effects) will result in only enough additional tax revenue to operate his profligate federal government for about eight (8) days! The actual number is 7.77 days, based upon projections of increased tax revenue of $81 billion from those individuals making more than $200,000 and couples making over $250,000, as a percentage of the requested expenditures in the Obama 2013 budget of $3.803 Trillion.

Obama completely ignores the actual history of tax reductions on tax revenues received and the progressivity of income tax rates. The facts are as follows: **"Every major marginal rate income tax cut of the last 50 years was followed by an unexpectedly large increase in tax revenues, a surge in taxes paid by the rich and a more progressive tax code—i.e., the share of taxes paid by the richest 1% rose."**[10]

Only two Democratic presidents—Woodrow Wilson and John F. Kennedy—have understood the fact that higher income tax rates on individuals and businesses do no automatically bring in higher tax revenues. At some point when tax rates increase, incomes begin to be invested in tax-free bonds, with the revenue reaping no federal taxes at all.

President John F. Kennedy stated it this way:

> A tax cut means higher family income and higher business profits and a balanced federal budget. . . . As the national income grows, the federal government will ultimately end up with more revenues. Prosperity is the real way to balance our budget. By lowering tax rates, by increasing jobs and income, we can expand tax revenues and finally bring our budget into balance. . .
>
> The final and best means of strengthening demand among consumers and business is to reduce the burden on private income and the deterrents to private initiative which are imposed by our present tax system . . . In short, it is a paradoxical truth that tax rates are too high today and tax revenues are too low and the soundest way to raise the revenues in the long run is to cut the rates now. . . . This country's own experience with tax reduction in 1954

has borne this out. And the reason is that only full employment can balance the budget, and tax reduction can pave the
way to that employment. The purpose of cutting taxes now is
not to incur a budget deficit, but to achieve the more
prosperous, expanding economy which can bring a budget
surplus. . . .

I repeat: our practical choice is not between a tax-cut
deficit and a budgetary surplus. It is between two kinds of
deficits: a chronic deficit of inertia, as the unwanted result of
inadequate revenues and a restricted economy; or a
temporary deficit of transition, resulting from a tax cut
designed to boost the economy, increase tax revenues, and
achieve—and I believe this can be done—a budget surplus.

The first type of deficit is a sign of waste and
weakness; the second reflects an investment in the future.[11]

—John F. Kennedy

What Obama has created, and what he continues to create
is, as JFK described it, "a chronic deficit of inertia, as the unwanted
result of . . . a restricted economy; . . . [which] deficit is a sign of
waste and weakness . . ."

Obama and his policies are wasteful and weak. They
restrict our economy and produce inertia by discouraging investors
and businesses from expanding because of every-increasing taxes
and regulations. The result is fewer jobs being created and
economic stagnation.

It becomes increasingly obvious that Obama is much more
interested in income redistribution than he is in job creation, the
American economy or low, middle or higher income taxpayers. In
his relentless push to give government more and more control over
our lives and to create more dependency upon government,
Obama refuses to even consider the lessons of history or
reasonable common-sense approaches that will help our economy
grow and produce millions of new jobs.

CHAPTER 5

WHY DOES OBAMA WANT TO CRIPPLE AMERICA?

There are disturbing facts about Obama that tell us much of the "why" behind Obama's hatred and intention to radically cripple the United States. Several books speak of these facts, including *The Anti-American President: Barack Hussein Obama*, available at: obamaexposed.com.

Virtually every adult who ever influenced Obama was a Marxist. His father's dream, which Obama says he inherited, was to replace capitalism and free enterprise with Marxist communism. That is who we now have at the head of our government!

From Obama's own book, *Dreams from My Father: A Story of Race and Inheritance*, we find insight into his mindset. NOTE: All of the quotations in the following paragraphs of this chapter are taken from Obama's book *Dreams from My Father: A Story of Race and Inheritance*.[12] Therefore, I will only provide page numbers in his book for them. He wrote that for this white-dominated American society he harbors a "**coil of rage**" (At p. 85) (emphasis added).

"**I ceased to advertise my mother's race at the age of 12 or 13, when I began to suspect that by doing so I was ingratiating myself to whites**" (Ibid., p. xv) (emphasis added).

"*White folks*. **The term itself was uncomfortable in my mouth at first; . . . It was obvious that certain whites could be exempted from the general category of our distrust. . . .** The term *white* was simply a shorthand for . . ., I decided, a tag for what my mother would call a bigot" (Ibid., 80-81, emphasis added).

"**There was something about him that made me wary, a little too sure of himself, maybe. And white**," he wrote of a white man in Chicago with whom he interviewed (Ibid., 142) (emphasis added).

In an article in *American Thinker*, Dr. John C. Drew speaks of his own former Marxist leanings and his meetings with and memory of Obama. Drew is an award-winning political scientist and a blogger at David Horowitz's NewReal Blog. Dr. Drew has taught political science and economics at Williams College.

Drew had received his diploma from Occidental College in 1979, "wearing the red armband that signified my solidarity with my Marxist brethren around the world . . ." He returned to Occidental College in 1980 to visit a friend, Caroline Boss, also a devoted Marxist. There, Boss introduced 19-year-old Obama and his friend, Mohammed Hasan Chandoo, a wealthy 21-year-old Pakistani student to Drew, saying, "They're on our side." In the discussion that followed, Drew expressed his vision of societal change being focused on winning elections. Drew recounts:

> **Boss and Obama, however, had a starkly different view. They believed that the economic stresses of the Carter years meant revolution was still imminent. The election of Reagan was simply a minor set-back in terms of the coming revolution. As I recall, Obama repeatedly used the phrase "When the revolution comes. . . . <u>There's going to be a revolution,</u>" Obama said, we need to be <u>organized and grow the movement. . . .</u>"**
>
> **. . . I responded it was unrealistic to think the working class would ever overthrow the capitalist system. As I recall, Obama reacted negatively to my critique, saying: "That's crazy!"** [13] (emphasis added).

Obama still believes that it will require severe economic stresses to bring about that "coming revolution." By creating more and more who are dependent on government for food stamps, welfare, unemployment, etc., Obama is actually creating ever greater economic stresses. Today, American cities are goind bankrupt because their expenses and commitments exceed their revenues. This trend will only worsen. Eventually, Obama's revolution will come in the same form of violent riots as we have recently seen in Greece. When city, state and federal governments cannot keep up with what increasing numbers of people who are dependent on governments have come to expect, violent revolution will be the inevitable result.

Drew is also quoted by Gary R. Jackson as he speaks of his first meeting with Obama at Occidental College:

> *. . I know something about what Barack Obama believed in 1980. At that time, the future president was a doctrinaire Marxist revolutionary . . .* [14]

In an interview with Paul Kengor, then guest-host on the Glen Meakem Program, a radio-talk show, Dr. Drew exposed Obama as a communist in these words:

> *As far as I can tell, I'm the only person in Obama's extended circle of friends who is willing to speak out and verify that he was a Marxist-Leninist in his sophomore year of college . . .* [15]

Think about it. If Obama, Sr., Bill Ayers, Jeremiah Wright or others like them were given the opportunity—without worry of later repercussions—to cripple America and do away with our capitalist, free enterprise system, wouldn't they do so? What about their sponge-like and doctrinaire follower—Obama?

CHAPTER 6

FURTHER EXPLANATION OF OBAMA'S MOTIVES

OBAMA'S DISDAIN FOR THE WISHES OF THE MAJORITY OF THE AMERICAN PEOPLE

"The essential feature of narcissistic personality disorder is a pervasive pattern of grandiosity . . . with a need for admiration and a lack of empathy for other people. . . ."
—Linda Bayer

"A lot of self-absorbed jerks are narcissists, but so are a lot of smooth, superficially charming, and charismatic people (who, unfortunately, are later revealed to be self-centered and dishonest)." —Jean M. Twenge and W. Keith Campbell

———————

Obama has consistently rejected outright the opinions and desires of the majority of the American people. His responses have shown a great disdain for the opinions of Americans. He ruthlessly attacks the motives and feelings of anyone who does not blindly agree with his opinions. He must always believe that his opinions are superior to anything anyone else can come up with.

Let's review certain personality disorders and compare them with Obama.

The essential feature of narcissistic personality disorder is a pervasive pattern of grandiosity—that is, an inflated sense of how important one is—along with a need

40

OBAMA'S 36 NEW AND HIGHER TAXES

for admiration and a lack of empathy for other people. . . .
Narcissistic people tend to exaggerate their abilities and
accomplishments, often appearing boastful or pretentious.[16]

Narcissistic people:

> see themselves as the center of the universe.　If you
> wish to have a relationship with one of them (and why
> would you?), you had better agree with him (sic). . . . They
> want to be pampered and admired; nothing else will meet
> their demanding expectations. . . . He will . . . win you
> with calculated too-good-to-be-true pseudo-charm, and
> then he will drain you dry.[17]

Other narcissistic characteristics include a:

> [p]reoccupation with fantasies of . . . brilliance, . . ., power,
> or limitless success, . . . [s]ense of entitlement, [e]xploitation
> of others to achieve goals . . .　[a]rrogance or haughtiness
> in attitude or behavior, [r]eluctance to accept blame or
> criticism, . . . [s]hallowness.[18]

> A narcissist is full of [him]self, has a big head, is a
> blowhard, loves the sound of his own voice, or is a legend in
> [his] own mind.
> A lot of self-absorbed jerks are narcissists, but so are
> a lot of smooth, superficially charming, and charismatic
> people (who, unfortunately, are later revealed to be self-
> centered and dishonest).[19]

Some narcissists are both self-absorbed jerks and smooth
and superficially charming and charismatic.

> People . . . whom we refer to as 'narcissists'—think
> they are better than others in social status, good looks,
> intelligence, and creativity.

However, they are not. . . . [N]arcissists see
themselves as fundamentally superior—they are
special, entitled, and unique. [In their own minds.]
. . . [They] use other people as pawns in a grand
game of deception. . . . Narcissists might brag about their
achievements (while blaming others for their shortcomings),
. . .   [who] constantly turn the conversation back to
themselves, manipulate and cheat to get ahead, . . .
with little concern for others, often manipulating and
exploiting people and viewing others as tools to make
themselves look and feel good.[20]

Even more than three and a half years into his presidency, Obama continues to tell the country how incredibly much he has achieved, while still blaming George W. Bush for his (Obama's) utter failure on the economy and nearly everything else.

Narcissists are arrogant and egotistical, even snobs. They expect special treatment and concessions from others and have an especially difficult time coping with criticism.

Does any of this sound familiar? Every one of the above-cited points fits Obama. Indeed, clinical narcissists often behave as does Obama. They have a serious mental disorder and find it extremely difficult understanding or acknowledging others' needs.

We may summarize and draw conclusions about Obama from the above and from the facts of Obama's childhood and adolescence. Thus, all Americans may evaluate the man to whom a majority of Americans have given such great power. That power has generally been misused.

Let's look at a few of the narcissistic "birds" that flock together with our focus—Obama: Rev. Wright, Bill Ayers, Van Jones. We will also look at several personality disorders. A number of writers, including some with psychiatric and psychoanalytical training and certifications, have looked at Obama's words, actions and aloofness, and have given their analyses. I will briefly describe some of these personality disorders, review Obama's weird and disabling childhood and then note some of the determinations of various experts concerning his resulting character disorders.

"Delusional disorder is characterized by a persistent 'non-bizarre' delusion—a delusion involving a phenomenon that the person's culture could conceivably regard as plausible."[21]

Delusionals look very normal, but their beliefs often (virtually always) vary from reality. They are unchangeable. Delusional cult leaders believe and claim they have extraordinary powers and/or intelligence. Those with a "messiah complex" are delusional. Their cult followers are also delusional enough to actually believe such nonsense about their phony "messiah" or any other cult leader. A DESCRIPTION OF ANY CURRENT PRESIDENT? A DESCRIPTION OF ANY "LAME-STREAM" MEDIA MEMBERS?

> Successful psychopaths . . . can charm you out of your heart, your knickers, and your trust fund before you know what is happening. Even when they disappear without a word, you may still staunchly defend them. It is their talent. . . Much like the narcissistic manipulator (and he may be both), the psychopath can be sinfully, stunningly charming, frequently highly intelligent, and again, too good to be true.[22]

Psychopaths can easily lie and remain calm, detached and appear normal, for they are such excellent liars. But they are anything but normal—they are the opposite of normal. For them, lying is almost more normal than telling the truth. Other people may feel stress when they lie, but not psychopaths.

I have reviewed the writings of numerous experts in the field of personality disorders. From multiple opinions, I have condensed and compiled a list of four things a human being needs to become a rational, normally-functioning adult. (1) He must feel loved. (2) He must be able to feel attachment to people. (3) He must have felt empathy from significant others for his own needs, suffering and fears in order to be able to feel empathy for others and their needs, suffering and fears. (4) He must have formed a solid and reasonable identity that develops from exposure to, and association with, examples of healthy role models. Obviously, numbers 1 through 3 can generally exist when number 4 does.

Obama's dysfunctional family and destructive upbringing stand in stark contrast to those four essential needs for an individual to be rational and normal. I will briefly review his childhood and youth. NOTE: As earlier done, all of the quotations in the following section of this chapter are taken from Obama's book *Dreams from My Father: A Story of Race and Inheritance*. Therefore, I will not provide individual citations for them.

Obama was first abandoned at age two by his adulterous, egotistical, alcoholic and Marxist father, Obama, Sr. Thereafter, his mother took him to Indonesia, where he lived with his mother, step-father and half-sister, Maya. His mother then hauled Obama back to the U. S. His half-sister, Maya, said they were "untethered . . . drifting in and out of worlds, here and there." Obama's unstable upbringing only got worse after that.

Obama's mother returned to Indonesia, but Obama refused to go. His mother abandoned and left him with his grandparents. Of this, Obama wrote, "I was to live with strangers." After run-ins with those grandparents, he said, "I'd arrived at an unspoken pact with my grandparents; I could live with them and they'd leave me alone so long as I kept my troubles out of sight."

So much for the first requirement to be a normally-functioning adult—"He must feel loved." So much for #2—"He must be able to feel attachment to people." So much as well for #3—"He must be able to feel empathy for others." No one close to Obama showed much, if any, true love for him. No one showed attachment to him. Everyone who should have cared abandoned him, physically and emotionally. Clearly, no one showed empathy for him. His wants, needs and fears seemed to have been completely ignored, as though they were unimportant to those others. He was never taught to feel empathy for anyone else. Instead, his role models showed him just the opposite. It appears that Obama has no understanding whatsoever of the concept.

Omit all of those three, and out goes #4 as well—"He must have formed a solid and reasonable identity that forms from exposure to, and association with, examples of healthy role models." His associations and role models look like what one would find in a horror movie. And the result was not healthy, either for Obama or for the country he would later come to "lead."

Obama's grandparents, with whom he lived, Stanley and Madelyn were abnormal themselves. Stanley's childhood was terrible. His dad abandoned his family. At age eight, Stanley discovered his dead mother, who had committed suicide. So Stanley was sent to his grandparents. He moved around, joined the military, and married Madelyn. Frustrated when their child was a girl—Obama's mother—he gave her his own first name, Stanley. After being ridiculed for her first name, Stanley began using her middle name, Ann.

Stanley drank heavily. He brought in Frank Marshall Davis, an admitted communist who worked for the Soviet Union, to be a mentor for Obama. Davis was an alcoholic, a racist, a pedophile and a misogynist. He authored the erotic book, *Sex Rebel: Black*.

Many knowledgeable people have publicly wondered if Davis abused Obama. Davis, who blamed racism and capitalism for all of the problems in society, deeply influenced Obama.

Obama observed and digested Davis' and his own father's mistrust of the system—the American capitalist system. Even though Obama lived a privileged life in Hawaii, he cultivated anger and resentment toward America in general, and whites, in particular. From high school on, Obama actively sought out people who reinforced and hardened his view of America, its economic system and the world. Included among these others are: socialists and Marxist professors at Occidental College; Rev.

Jeremiah Wright—a strongly anti-America pastor; Bill Ayers—an admitted and unrepentant terrorist; Marcus—a Black Panther who felt rage against white domination; Louis Farrakhan—the radical anti-American leader of the Nation of Islam; and Michelle—his wife, who publicly declared that prior to an Obama 2008 campaign victory, she had never before in her adult life felt pride in her country, America. This was despite her own privileged life.

Louis Farrakhan, amazingly, even labeled Obama the Messiah![23] How ridiculous, yet frightening. Such drivel could only have the effect of increasing Obama's own false pride and delusions of grandeur—and they are delusions.

Obama's dysfunctional family and destructive upbringing stand in stark contrast to those four essential needs for an individual to be rational and normal. So all four of the needs and requirements for the development of a normal adult appear to have been absent from Obama's childhood and adolescence.

As many have concluded, with what should have been an extremely embarrassing childhood and adolescence, Obama had a choice to make. (1) He could choose to face the truth about his life—and about his parents, grandparents and others who raised and influenced him. This would be the wise but difficult choice. It could be embarrassing for him. Or, (2) he could save face—by lying to himself and all others—and blaming whites, the United States, Western Europe, and everyone else for all of his family's problems. He could blame everyone for his own numerous problems—everyone he deemed unlike himself or an obstacle to getting whatever he might want. He could likewise blame everyone else for his own feelings of inferiority, his paranoia, his narcissism and for the wrongs he has "suffered" at the hands of white America and the western nations.

The second option—the one he chose to believe and live—resulted in his blind and false conclusions about himself and those around him. His father did not want to abandon him—racism and colonialism made him do it. His mother did not leave him of her own will—America and white society forced it. Obama's grandparents did not destroy his proper perspective by permitting a corrupt man like Frank Marshall Davis prolonged association with him. They were just being normal "white folks."

Just as nothing his parents did was their fault, Obama blamed everything he did not like upon whites and America as a whole. In doing this, Obama never had to accept blame for any of his or his family's folly. He never had to be accountable for anything. Everything was someone else's fault. And still today, when he does not get what he wants, his smiling face turns mean, and he lashes out with junkyard dog fury against anyone who stands in the path of his getting his way. He appears stuck in childhood, wanting every toy he sees—whether it is his or not. Because he wants them all, he "must" be entitled to them.

Moreover, he appears insistent that he create a mass of people who are "entitled" to have others provide for. Others should do so, for those others—white, independent and affluent Americans—are to blame for all of the problems and unrealized wants of society (and his newly created "entitleds").

It is a screwed up mentality, but it is quite easy to see why he holds onto it. After all, society forced his parents and others to cram it down his throat!

Why include the above description of Obama? Because it may at least partially explain why he does not care about what the majority of American citizens want. In fact, not only does he not care, he may be so self-absorbed that any opinion which does not match his own will not even penetrate his closed mind. Clearly, what Americans need is not anywhere near as important to Obama as what he wants.

Unless one is willing to ignore the obvious truth, it is absolutely easy to see the incompetent, intentionally and malignantly evil being foisted on our country by Obama and his minions. The wishes and opinions of the majority of Americans simply do not matter to Obama.

CHAPTER 7

WHY DOES OBAMA WANT TO RAISE TAXES?

"A government which robs Peter to pay Paul can always depend on the support of Paul."   —George Bernard Shaw

"I contend that for a nation to try to tax itself into prosperity is like a man standing in a bucket and trying to lift himself up by the handle."   —Sir Winston Churchill

"The stimulus package just raised higher the cliff from which we all will have to jump off."
                —New York's Democratic Lt. Governor, Richard Ravitch

—————————————————

One of the major reasons Obama wants to raise your taxes is that he wants government to control every part of the U. S. economy. Part of that means that government will need to spend much more so that more people will become dependent on assistance from the government. Obviously, those who are so dependent will support and vote for candidates who promise to keep that government assistance flowing.

The so-called 2009 federal "stimulus" bill was supposed to resolve the financial crisis. It absolutely did not! It only made it worse. As New York's Democratic Lt. Governor, Richard Ravitch stated, "The stimulus package just raised higher the cliff from which we all will have to jump off."[24]

Why can't Obama and congressional Democrats figure that out? Or do they simply not care?

A short, cute story (cute at least initially) will help bring understanding of how Obama is using his support from the radical Democrats in Congress and the blind "lame-stream" media to keep the American people from revolting against his short-sighted, destructive agenda. The story was originally told by an unidentified teacher. I have modified it slightly to fit my format. I'll entitle it, "Can We Really Afford the Ice Cream?"

From a teacher: We are worried about "The Cow" when it is all about the "Ice Cream."

The most eye-opening lesson in politics I ever had was while teaching third grade this year. The 2008 presidential election was heating up and some of the children showed an interest. I decided we would have an election for class president. The class would choose the nominees. They would make a campaign speech and the class would vote.

To simplify the process, candidates were nominated by other class members. We discussed what kinds of characteristics these students should have. We got many nominations and from those, John and Mary were picked to run for the top spot.

The class had done a great job in their selections. Both candidates were good kids. I thought John might have an advantage because he had a lot of parental support. I had never seen Mary's mother.

The day arrived for them to make their speeches. John went first. He had specific ideas about how to make our class a better place. He ended by promising to do his very best. Every one applauded. He sat down and Mary came to the podium.

Mary's speech was concise. She said, "If you elect me, I will give you ice cream." She sat down. The class went wild. "Yes! Yes! We want ice cream!"

    She surely would say more. She did not have to.
A discussion followed. How did she plan to pay for the
ice cream? She wasn't sure.

    Would her parents buy it or would the class pay for
it. She didn't know.

    The class really didn't care. They only thought of
ice cream.

    John was forgotten. Mary won by a landslide.[25]

End of that fairy tale. Let's move on to the next—not a fairy tale, but it certainly is fiction—nightmarish—and yet unfortunately real-life.

Every time Barack Obama opens his mouth, if he doesn't attack the "rich" or those who oppose him, he offers ice cream. Nearly fifty percent of the people react like nine-year-olds. They want ice cream. The other fifty percent know they're going to have to feed the cow and clean up the mess.

The wise Rev. William John Henry Boetcker, a twentieth century Presbyterian minister and noted public speaker wrote the following statements that bear repeating. (Many have incorrectly attributed this quotation to Abraham Lincoln. It is wise enough that it is something he could well have said.)

    You cannot bring about prosperity by discouraging thrift.
    You cannot strengthen the weak by weakening the strong.
    You cannot help little men by tearing down big men.
    You cannot lift the wage earner by pulling down the wage payer.
    You cannot help the poor by destroying the rich.
    You cannot establish sound security on borrowed money.
    You cannot further the brotherhood of man by inciting class hatred.
    You cannot keep out of trouble by spending more than you earn.
    You cannot build character and courage by destroying men's initiative and independence.

You cannot help men permanently by doing for them what they can and should do for themselves.[26]

Reading Rev. Boetcker's brilliant words refute nearly everything Obama has said and done. Rev. Boetcker's statements are so full of insight, one would think he was speaking today. I truly wish he were. But we can take his wise words, written some 95 years ago, and apply them to ourselves and our country today. Since Obama certainly will not, we must find someone else who will also show (not just feign) such wisdom.

Beyond just offering ice cream, Obama promises it in great quantities. What he delivers is never as promised. He promises the moon, and having delivered nothing close, he then tells us how fully he performed and kept his promise. When he speaks, he expects everyone to deny reality and accept whatever he says, as though his saying something makes it so. The problem is, it doesn't. But he keeps right on talking—ad nauseum—repeatedly expecting everyone to ignore his previously undelivered promises.

Another wise man and President, Gerald R. Ford, gave us a short, yet profound truth. He said, **"A government big enough to give you everything you want is a government big enough to take from you everything you have."**[27]

Obama has to know that is true. The problem is it appears that such a government with a weak economy is exactly what he wants to bring about. Remember Dr. John Drew's account of Obama's hankering for a revolution in our country. Destroying our economy would certainly help lead to exactly that. It is astonishing to me that any sane person could want that for our country. Maybe no sane person does!

If by chance, he actually does not know the truth—he really knows nothing about economics or how to lead a nation to prosperity and is unfit to lead a great country such as ours.

The next two short quotations are also many times wiser than anything Obama has proposed—and more importantly—than anything he has done. The first comes from Winston Churchill,

British Prime Minister during the decisive part of World War II. He stated,

> **I contend that for a nation to try to tax itself into prosperity is like a man standing in a bucket and trying to lift himself up by the handle.**[28]

Obama's intention has always been to raise taxes. As I previously wrote, if Republicans had not trounced the Democrats in the November 2010 election, retaking control of the House and expanding their numbers in the Senate, the Bush-era tax cuts would never have been extended. They were extended—but only until 2013. So those cut taxes will increase, with many other additional taxes that are scheduled to strike all Americans—thanks to Obama.

The second quotation is given to us by George Bernard Shaw. **"A government which robs Peter to pay Paul can always depend on the support of Paul."**[29]

Obama's approach is one of class warfare. He has always pitted the poor and those who live off of entitlements against "the rich." The "rich," of course, are businesses, banks, and people who make enough to take the risk of investing in businesses that create jobs. Obama never ceases to demagogue them. The poor and other "entitleds" are the "Pauls." Obama clearly has their support. In fact, there are millions of "Pauls" who wholeheartedly support Obama. And Obama, without deserved shame, eagerly seeks to rob more and more Peters.

Most of what Obama has said and done has had precisely the opposite effect from what our country needs. The effect has consistently been opposite from what Obama has said would happen. I have come to know that we cannot trust that what he says is really what he intends to do. Nor can anyone believe what he says the results will actually be. It is hard to know if he is simply saying what he believes is needed to get what he wants—which often appears to be the case. Or does he truly believe his policies will actually bring about what our country needs—which is never the case. There is always a disconnect between what he says and does and what our country actually needs. Some examples follow.

1 – Obama's initial addresses to Congress were intended to restore confidence. Instead, consumers reduced spending and investors sold and decreased their investing.

2 – When Obama's Treasury Secretary put forth his bank plan supposedly to relieve uncertainty, the actual result was that the plan added to uncertainty among bankers and investors.

3 – After virtually every Obama speech aimed to encourage investment, business investors determined they had better hold back on expansion and further investment.

As is stated above, it appears that Obama's true intention is to drive the U. S. economy into the ground, and he is just stating otherwise to keep everyone from rebelling against him. If he actually believes his agenda will help our country, then he is naïve and incompetent. The truth is that his agenda will keep our economy from recovering, or at best, severely slow any potential recovery. In the long term, his foolish and out-of-control spending policies will truly bring our country to bankruptcy.

Many current projections show unemployment rising to nine percent or higher in 2013 if Obama gets his tax increases on "the rich." That alone should keep intelligent people from voting for him.

You may believe that he does not intend to destroy our country and its economy. Is he just naïve—or worse—clueless? Let us analyze his agenda and the means he has used to put it in place. Then each can decide what he really is and what his true intentions are.

Obama's agenda has a two-fold focus: (1) The short-term focus is to gain political and public (if not business) acceptance; and (2) The long-term goal is to radically change America. His position from before his 2008 campaign to the present time has always been to bring about change. He said that he intends to "transform America."

Investors and business men and women, by contrast, look to determine whether or not to immediately do something to meet a short-term need. Their primary focus is on the long-term impact of what is now in place, or what is now being put in place. They DO NOT want America to be radically changed. They want continued freedom, both personal and business, non-confiscatory taxes and the real (not just falsely promised) opportunity for economic growth.

OBAMA'S AND BUSINESSES' LONG-TERM GOALS ARE DIAMETRICALLY OPPOSED TO EACH OTHER! MOREOVER, OBAMA'S FOCUS AND MOST AMERICANS' DESIRES ARE ALSO DIAMETRICALLY OPPOSED TO EACH OTHER!

When Obama declares his plan, he hopes the short-term effect will be that it plays well with most in the media and the general public. But as investors examine what the impact on them and their business will be down the road, they cringe and hold back. Why? Because they actually know something about business and what it takes to have one succeed. Obama has never run a business. He has hardly ever even had a real job. If he knows anything at all about how to help businesses succeed—which would produce jobs—he has not shown it or done it in any way. Sometimes he talks a good talk (as long as he has his teleprompter and does not reveal any true details). If he deals in platitudes, he sounds good—well, so long as he is not proposing what he truly wants. But when the details come out, business people and risk-taking investors run for cover.

As we know, in his first address to Congress, he unveiled his plan for a trillion-dollar health care plan—obamacare. Under that plan, the federal government will basically take over financial responsibility for a child from birth to its graduation from college. This would include universal health care, universal pre-school, universal elementary and higher education. To many—especially those who would be receiving the freebies—this sounded great. It sounded like buckets and buckets of ice cream! All of the "Pauls" in our country were excited. Obama had their support. All of the Peters feared for their skins, for they will be paying for all of it.

In fact, obamacare has already put such increases in place. At the same time, he assures anyone gullible enough to believe him, that he will create millions of new jobs. His statements and policies are as likely to produce the results our country needs, including millions of new jobs, as if he were to say that he and his policies will keep everyone warm. Then he proceeds to confiscate everyone's coat. His statements and policies fly in the face of Winston Churchill's truism quoted earlier. **Obama insists he will tax our nation into prosperity. Obama's notion is truly "like a man standing in a bucket and trying to lift himself up by the handle."** Reality contradicts Obama.

When we realistically consider the consequences of his "ice cream in the sky" plans, it becomes frightening. Obama's annual federal budgets increased discretionary spending by twenty-four percent in only 18 months in office! We now regularly incur annual trillion dollar plus deficits.

One telling set of comparative facts is simply hard to believe—but the numbers are true. During President Clinton's time in office, the deficit increased on average by $547 million per day. During George W. Bush's time in office, the average daily increase was $1.6 billion. During Obama's first 30 months in office, the deficit increased on average by $4.1 billion PER DAY! I find it impossible to believe that any reasonable person can feel the federal government under Obama is not spending too much or that Obama is doing anything right for the American economy.

This growing national debt and deficit spending will certainly bring a crisis of confidence in our own currency, lead to hyper-inflation and wipe out the middle class. Obama claims he is fighting for the middle class. The truth is he is systematically destroying it. His excessive spending will seriously harm businesses and increase unemployment. It will require enormous additional borrowing from the Chinese (giving them greater and greater influence over us). Plus, each time Obama's Federal Reserve chairman has "bought" U. S. debt with IOUs created out of "thin air," world oil prices have gone up. Why? Because Middle Eastern oil producing countries know that with each such phony quantitative easing, the U. S. dollar becomes worth less. It is becoming more and more certain that inflation resulting from our government printing so much money will devour us. As inflation increases, low- and middle-income Americans will be less able to afford many necessities.

Obama's horrendous cap and trade legislation (often referred to as "cap and tax" by those who know what it actually would do) will make little difference in any world climate change, but would do an incredible amount of harm to the U. S. economy and families. U. S. businesses would pay many billions more in taxes each year. Individual taxpayers would pay thousands more each year because of the monstrous costs this taxing legislation would impose. Senator Jim Inhofe, of Oklahoma, provided evidence in his speech on the Senate floor that Obama's proposed cap and trade legislation would have added *"$6.735 trillion into the system in the form of higher energy costs to get back an estimated $802 billion in tax relief. That's a return of only $1.00 for every $8.40 paid."*[30]

In other words, taxpayers would pay $8.40 in new and increased taxes and only receive $1 in benefits. The greedy Obama government would get the remaining $7.40 in taxpayers' hard-earned money.

Obama's corporate tax plan has the very same lame approach. His announced intention is to tax multi-national companies that "export jobs to other countries." In the short term and on its face, this sounds like a great way to get bundles of tax money, with no cost to Americans. But again, either Obama really does want the U. S. economy to collapse or he has no clue about the true consequences or how businesses and economies work. If, in fact, he wants the U. S. economy to collapse, then he knows his corporate tax plan will literally help bring that about. If he does not know that, we need to elect someone who knows what he is doing. This is what real effect his short-sighted plan would have.

American corporations with foreign subsidiaries already pay taxes in those other countries. If we required them to pay higher taxes here, one or both of two things would be the result: (1) Their expenses, increased by extra taxes, will make them uncompetitive both in the United States and in those foreign countries. To make any profits, they would be required to raise their prices, driving customers to lower-priced, foreign competitors; and (2) Multi-national corporations with operations or factories in the U. S. will simply leave and relocate in less overbearing countries with more intelligent governments. The ultimate consequence of either of the two initial results—U. S. companies becoming uncompetitive or of multi-nationals leaving—will be the loss of millions of existing jobs. The second ultimate consequence will be fewer, not more new jobs. The third ultimate consequence will be fewer, not more tax dollars to a greedy, yet clueless government. It should be easy to see how disastrous Obama's agenda is.

Using the same logic—actually the same absence of logic— Obama has said he intends to sharply raise taxes on all investment income. This includes dividends, interest and capital gains.

During an April 16, 2008 Democratic presidential debate, Obama disclosed a major tenet of his socialist mindset by explaining his view on tax-policy "fairness." When asked by moderator Charlie Gibson if he would favor a cut in the capital gains rate if it led to higher revenues as it did during previous administrations, **Obama said: "Well, Charlie, what I've said is that I would look at raising the capital gains tax for purposes of fairness."** So he would not cut capital gains tax rates even if it would bring in more tax revenues for his excessive spending! His skewed view of "fairness" is more important to him than a healthy and growing economy with millions of more jobs for Americans.

Obama's foolish approach to grossly expand government into every part of American life completely contradicts the wisdom expressed by Thomas Jefferson:

> **A wise and frugal government . . . shall leave [the people] free to regulate their own pursuits of industry and improvement and shall not take from the mouth of labor the bread it has earned. This is the sum of good government . . .**
>
> **I predict future happiness for Americans if they can <u>prevent the government from wasting the labors of the people under the pretense of taking care of them.</u>**[31]

What Obama plans to do is not to lift or expand the economy. His plan is to rob more and more from the "Peters" to give additional amounts to more and more "Pauls". In so doing, Obama will rob both the "Peters" and the "Pauls." From the "Peters," he will steal the capital and incentive to invest and work to start and expand job-creating businesses. As to the "Pauls," he will cripple them by robbing them of their motivation to work and to be independent, as well as of their deserved satisfaction and pride that come from providing for themselves. He will have created millions of non-achievers who are wholly dependent upon a greedy and power-hungry government, for there will be millions fewer productive jobs created or available in the private sector.

Obama's accelerated Marxist agenda fits exactly what Ronald Reagan described as the socialist belief. He stated that socialist agenda this way:

> **The American people will never knowingly adopt socialism. But under the name of "liberalism"**

they will adopt every fragment of the socialist program until one day America will be a socialist nation, without knowing how it happened.[32]

Approximately two-thirds of all new jobs are created by small businesses. Most of the rest are created by large businesses. **Productive jobs are NOT created by government.** With no disrespect to the poor, virtually no **jobs are created by poor people**. They can barely afford to feed, clothe and house themselves. Jobs are created by people who have enough money to invest. **So the dumbest thing a politician can do if he wants to have more jobs created, is to destroy the incentive to take risks by increasing the tax drain on dollars available or used for investment.** Doing so will simply shrink the available investment funds and discourage investment which will result in fewer new businesses and decreased business expansion. Both mean fewer new jobs created. That means less net tax revenues. It is really very simple. But it is apparently too complex for Obama or the Democrats in Congress to grasp.

The fact is, to do that which will reduce the very things needed to bring about new job creation is folly. It is disastrous socialism. It is the path to destroy our country. It is anti-American. But it is Obama's way.

I have explained the new taxes resulting from Obama's sordid push to take over the U. S. health insurance industry through obamacare. The requirements in that monstrosity, although continually denied by lies from its Democratic pushers—Obama, Harry Reid, Pelosi and other Democrats—will certainly result in one or both of two things: (1) Require insurance companies to ruinously change their coverage and American citizens' access to the high level of health care we currently have in our country; and (2) Make insurers subject to the federal government's takeover of their companies, and all health care in the United States. It is precisely not what America needs. Full discussion of obamacare's consequences warrants its own book because it is such an enormous and disastrous anti-business, anti-economic-growth and anti-health-care law. It will certainly result in less and lower-quality health care.

Obama simply cannot be unaware that his policies are bringing about the opposite from what most American citizens ultimately want and what our country truly needs. Whether because of malignantly evil and intentional actions or sheer incompetence, the disastrous end is the same. Innocent people and our country are being seriously harmed, and will hereafter continue to be seriously harmed. Obama's intentional and evil, or clueless and incompetent policies against American businesses will destroy many of them—the very lifeblood of America and of its citizens' prosperity and freedom.

CHAPTER 8

CONCLUSION

What Obama is actually saying as he campaigns is: The economy I inherited was in bad shape. [And it was.] I (Obama) have not been able to do much to change it for the better in my first 3 ½ years in office. Won't you please re-elect me and during the next four years I will do the very same things that have not worked in my first 3 ½ years!

———————————

Obama and the Democrats desperately want to keep Americans' focus off of the pathetic and incompetent job he has done. They also hope American voters do not realize before November 2012's election that he and they are fully responsible for 36 new and higher taxes that will be extremely destructive for the American economy. He has already severely crippled our nation's economy.

Obama and congressional Democrats have "blown the roof off" in unnecessary and worthless spending. Our country's spiraling debt portends disastrous consequences for the future, and not just the distant future.

Barack Obama has fought and sought to cripple our country's free-enterprise system. In words and policies, he has done so much to demonize and restrict businesses, large and small. His policies have had numerous horrendous results for our economy. Unemployment has skyrocketed and has remained unacceptably high after more than three and a half years of his destructive administration. There are over 22 million under-employed and unemployed Americans!

Because Obama's agenda creates market uncertainty, oppressive regulations and excessive taxation, existing businesses have not expanded or made significant investments that would create new jobs. Many potential new businesses have not been started, due to the same poor economy and businessmen's certainty that it will not improve during Obama's administration. Obama's anti-business rhetoric and policies have kept, and will continue to keep, investors on the sidelines. There is both uncertainty and certainty about the economy, as contradictory as that may sound. Businesses and investors are uncertain that the economic climate will allow them to recoup any investment with a reasonable profit. But they are certain that this president and the Democrats in Congress either do not know how, or do not want, to develop a national climate conducive to economic growth and prosperity.

During Obama's short tenure, we have seen the near nationalization or the effectual taking control of large segments of our economy—the auto industry, the mortgage industry, student loans and health care. The financial sector has become much more restricted and controlled by Obama's federal government.

Obama and his cronies in Congress seem oblivious to what our country and its economy really need. Their actions appear to be intended to wrest total control of most aspects of our country's economy. If they are allowed to succeed, our country and our freedoms will be destroyed. The U. S. will become as pathetic and oppressive as the former Soviet Union.

Obamacare, like socialized medicine wherever it has been implemented, will cost more than our current health care system and more than our economy and taxpayers can afford to pay. But the actual health care it will provide, like other socialized health care systems, will be of lesser quality. Rationing of many types of medical care will absolutely become necessary. Significant delays in receiving treatment and surgery will result. Its many new and increased taxes and repressive regulations will severely impact most Americans and businesses. Those affected include but are not limited to: employees, employers, doctors and other health care providers, insurance companies and taxpayers. Most of all, it will negatively impact patients and the care they receive.

Obamacare's new and increased ones are already striking America's businesses and individuals. As shown in earlier chapters, obamacare mandates at least 22 new and higher taxes. At least another fourteen new or higher taxes are also part of the destructive legacy of Obama.

Obama's desires for "cap and trade" ("cap and tax") have been thwarted in Congress. But, unwilling to accept "no" for an answer, this narcissist seeks as many of its onerous restrictions as possible through administrative regulations.

He is always overwhelmingly divisive in his rhetoric and actions toward everyone who disagrees with him. Either one agrees with him, or that person (or group) is his enemy. His junk-yard-dog approach toward his enemies—at least within the U. S., has followed the Saul Alinsky, community organizer approach: to freeze and isolate, then demonize (attack) them to destroy their effectiveness. Alinsky wrote:

> **The devil challenged authority and got his own kingdom, and that goes to the heart of what [the] left is really about. That of course is to get power any way you can, including lying, cheating and stealing. The ultimate rule is that the ends justify the means.**[33]

Hmmmm. Who else do we know who was a community organizer and who follows those Alinsky's rules? Obama never hesitates to say one thing and then do the exact opposite. That certainly follows Alinsky's rule. Obama cannot be trusted.

In his own words, he clearly has adopted as his own his father's beliefs. His father's feelings included hatred of America, other Western nations and the free-market system. Obama has embraced his father's desire for Marxist-Leninist socialism. Many of those with whom Obama has associated throughout his adult life are America-haters. If one wanted to bring America down to her knees, that person would basically follow the same course Obama has taken. He continues today on that same course.

Even if saner minds prevail, and Obama and his Democratic cronies in Congress are booted out in 2012, there will still remain many problems brought on by Obama and today's congressional Democrats. Because of the destructive things they have done to our entire country, it will be extremely difficult, if possible at all, to fully undo the damage. It will be difficult at best to get our nation's unemployed back into productive jobs, our economy on a prosperous path and our country's overpowering debt under control. But Obama's reelection will bring disaster.

The disastrous things briefly mentioned in the above paragraphs are the true legacy of this anti-American president. Hopefully, that legacy will not also include the total collapse of the United States' economy.

His cult followers will seek to explain away what their idol has written and said. They will seek to excuse his words and policies by moving the focus away from him and onto others. They will criticize the factual things written about Obama. But to do so, they must deny and distort the truth. What he has said absolutely cannot be honestly or reasonably explained away. He and others may try to push it aside, change the subject, or cover it up. They may seek to dodge having to answer for it by going on the offensive, to "attack the messenger." They will almost certainly still try to blame George W. Bush, to somehow justify the despicable things said and done by Obama. But they cannot truthfully say that Obama did not write or say what he, in fact, wrote and said. They can try to "spin it" or dismiss and gloss over it. Most Americans are too smart to swallow such cunning lies.

Hopefully, most Americans will have the chance to read or hear and understand most of the truths shown herein about him and his radical, anti-American feelings, and the horrendously destructive new and higher taxes he already has in place. That will be the only chance our country has to correct its current wrong course and to put someone in the White House who actually loves America. Only then will we have someone who will work to strengthen America and pull her out of her current tailspin. That tailspin has us heading into a disastrous economic ravine. We need someone to set America on an upward course once again.

Many who read and understand the destructive words and policies of Obama will see them for what they are—disastrous for our country and our freedoms. Some will find it hard to believe that he could possibly be intentionally seeking to harm our country. Most of the time, he comes across as nice, even likeable—when he is not in attack-dog mode.

I find it impossible to believe that he could be doing all of the things presented in this book without knowing exactly what he is doing. He can only fulfill the dreams he got from his father—dreams he has fully adopted and made his own—by pursuing the course laid out for him by his father. Those dreams from his father include a hatred for western nations, the leader of which is the United States, and a desire to replace our capitalist economic system with a Marxist one. In the socialist, Marxist mold, businesses are the enemy and government is the hero. Government can only control and provide for the citizenry after businesses and their power have been eliminated. Obama has clearly expressed his desire and intention to transform our country. The kind of transformation he seeks has been exposed by his words and policies thus far. He wants redistribution of wealth—a socialist/Marxist concept. He has already made great strides toward government's taking over or controlling several of the most significant segments of our economic system.

If re-elected, his true self will not need to remain hidden as it must now be. Until after the 2012 presidential election, Obama must appear innocent and middle-of-the-road ideologically. If re-elected, he will return to the radical, socialist left with a vengeance—the vengeance he inherited from his father. The transformation he seeks will not improve America. It will turn our country more and more into the distorted and destructive socialist vision he adopted from his father.

It is remotely possible that Obama is innocently doing all these destructive things out of sheer ignorance and incompetence. I do not believe he is that naïve or dumb. I do not see any innocence in him.

Remember Obama's belief as related by Dr. John C. Drew:

> **. . . The election of Reagan was simply a minor set-back in terms of the coming revolution. As I recall, <u>Obama repeatedly used the phrase[s] There's going to be a revolution," . . . "When the revolution comes</u> . . . "we need to be organized and grow the movement. . . ."** I distinctly remember Obama surprising me by bringing up Frantz Fanon [a French revolutionary who favored Marxism] and **colonialism**. He impressed me with his knowledge of these two topics . . . [Remember, Obama, Sr.'s focus and hatred were directed at the colonizing countries and he recommended certain anti-American socialist and Marxist books that Obama has read.]
>
> Boss and **Obama** seemed to think their ideological purity was a persuasive argument in **predicting that <u>a coming revolution would end capitalism</u>**.
>
> . . . I know something about what **Barack Obama** believed in 1980. At that time, the future president **was a doctrinaire Marxist revolutionary**, . . .[34] (emphasis added).

Obama's college-day desire for revolution lives on in him today. That was the major dream he took from his father. His words and actions show he is still pursuing that revolution to "transform" America. He will do this through numerous new and excessive taxes, onerous regulations and ridiculous and irresponsible spending.

Obviously, if he were to announce his real intentions, there would be revolt by the vast majority of our citizens. He has achieved and put in place as much of the transformation he seeks as he could possibly do since taking office. The 2010 midterm shellacking the Republicans handed the Democrats in Congress has clearly slowed down his inexorable march toward complete socialist transformation of our country. But his re-election would prevent the revocation of the most malignant parts of the transformation already in place. That would be disastrous to us and to the liberty we enjoy. It would eliminate our liberty to pursue happiness in the way we choose and reap the rewards of our own hard work and financial risk. It will restrict even our religious liberty.

The greatness of America is the goodness of her citizens. The quotation, sometimes attributed to de Tocqueville says it best: **"America is great because she is good. If America ceases to be good, America will cease to be great."**[35]

Radical left (so-called "progressive") parties and governments, including our own, falsely claim they are taking certain peoples' money to help others less fortunate. **They—the radical left—are actually weakening the capable and crippling the less capable**. Government's taking is a dictatorial counterfeit for voluntary individual charity. When a government takes too much from some of its people—misleadingly saying it is to do more for the people—that government is becoming more and more like a repressive Marxist state—the former Soviet Union. Those claims sounded noble then as they do now. But the result is the farthest thing from noble. It is autocratic dictatorship, with the greatest costs being the loss of both freedom and the motivation to improve oneself. The power that enables America to do the good it does around the world and to be the strongest and most prosperous nation on earth is the freedom from governmental interference in our citizens' right to morally and legally pursue happiness. May these things never be forgotten or lost.

Remember the socialists' belief, secretly advocated by Obama and other liberals in America today as quoted earlier:

> The American people will never knowingly adopt ocialism. But under the name of "liberalism" they will adopt every fragment of the socialist program until one day America will be a socialist nation, without knowing how it happened.[36]

Jefferson warned us against exactly what Obama is doing. Obama continues to take (tax) more and more "under the pretense of taking care of the people."

What Obama is actually saying as he campaigns is: The economy I inherited was in bad shape. [And it was.] I (Obama) have not been able to do anything to change it for the better in my first 3 ½ years in office. Won't you please re-elect me and during the next four years I will do the very same things that have not worked in my first 3 ½ years!

We need real—and effective—change, now more than ever before, but not "ice cream in the sky" change. We need: (1) change that will create an economic and tax climate which encourages individuals and businesses to expand and create new jobs; (2) change that will once again bring international respect for the U. S.; (3) change that will not bankrupt our country; and (4) change that will help us believe once more that things will actually improve. I sincerely hope and pray that this will come very soon to the country I love. It is obvious that it will not come from Obama.

May God bless America and those who love her and appreciate the freedoms she provides—including freedom from the tyranny of their own government.

SOURCES

[1] S. Jackson, "Obama relegates Republicans 'to the back of the bus.'", *Free Republic*, October 26, 2010, http://www.freerepublic.com/focus/f-news/2614725/posts.

[2] Kengor, Paul, "Dreams from Frank Marshall Davis," *American Thinker*, October 30, 2008, www.americanthinker.com/2008/10/dreams from frank marshall day.html, October 30, 2008.

[3] Barack H. Obama, Sr., "Problems Facing Our Socialism," East Africa Journal, http://www.politico.com/static/PPM41 eastafrica.html, 3, July 1965.

[4] List of new or higher taxes from various federal government publications of legislation, including "Patient Protection and Affordable Care Act," passed March 21, 2010 and "Health Care and Education Reconciliation Act of 2010," passed March 25, 2010 and Tax Relief, Unemployment Insurance Reauthorization and Job Creation Act of 2010, passed Dec. 17, 2010.

[5] Updated Estimates of the "Impact of the Coverage Provisions of PPACA and the Reconciliation Act," made in March 2011, pgs. 6, 12, 13, et seq., http://www.cbo.gov/ftpdocs/121xx/doc12119/03-30-HealthCareLegislation.pdf. Additional Information on the new and higher taxes of obamacare can be found at http://www.gpo.gov/fdsys/pkg/PLAW-111publ148/content-detail.html.

[6] Additional information on the new and higher taxes of obamacare can be found at: http://www.gpo.gov/fdsys/pkg/CREC-2010-03-24/pdf/CREC-2010-03-24-pt1-PgS1923-9.pdf.

[7] Quotation from Ronald Wilson Reagan, 41st President of the United States of America.

[8] Franklin, Benjamin, American founding father and elder statesman.

[9] See http://www.bizjournals.com/charlotte/blog/morning-edition/2012/07/ernst-young-raising-taxes-on.html.

[10] "The Romney Hood Fairy Tale: The false, invented analysis behind Obama's tax claims," *The Wall Street Journal*, Review & Outlook, http://online.wsj.com/article/SB10000872396390443792604577574910276629448.html.

[11] Kennedy, John F., Address and Question and Answer Period at the Economic Club of New York, December 14, 1962, http://www.presidency.ucsb.edu/ws/index.php?pid=9057.

[12] Obama, Barack, *Dreams from My Father: A Story of Race and Inheritance*, (New York, Three Rivers Press), 1995, 2004. The various quotations are taken from the following pages of said book: 85; xv; 80-81; 142.

[13] John Drew, "Meeting Young Obama," *American Thinker*, http://www.americanthinker.com/2011/02/meeting_oung_obama.html, July 28, 2011, originally dated February 24, 2011.

[14] Gary P. Jackson, "A Time For Choosing," February 25, 2011, http://thespeechatimeforchoosing.wordpress.com/2011/02/25/john-drew-meeting-young-barack-obama-marxist-revolutionary/.

[15] Kengor, Paul, "Dreams from Frank Marshall Davis," *American Thinker*, www.americanthinker.com/2008/10/dreams from frank marshall day.html, October 30, 2008.

[16] Bayer, Linda, Ph.D., *The Encyclopedia of Psychological Disorders - Personal Disorders*, (Philadelphia, Chelsea House Publishers, 2000), 59.

[17] McCoy, Dorothy, Ed.D., *The Manipulative Man*, (Avon, MA, Adams Media, 2006), 7.

[18] Ibid., 169, 170.

[19] Jean M. Twenge, Ph.D., and W. Keith Campbell, Ph.D., *The Narcissism Epidemic Living in the Age of Entitlement*, (New York, Free Press 2009), 18.

[20] Ibid., 19.

[21] Bayer, Linda, Ph.D., *The Encyclopedia of Psychological Disorders - Personal Disorders*, (Philadelphia, Chelsea House Publishers, 2000), 8.

[22] McCoy, Dorothy, Ed.D., *The Manipulative Man*, (Avon, MA, Adams Media, 2006), 8.

[23] "Farrakhan on Obama: 'The Messiah is absolutely speaking,' Barack has captured the youth,' will bring about 'universal change,'" *World Net Daily*, posted October 9, 2008, http://www.wnd.com/?pageId=77539.

[24] New York's Democratic Lt. Governor, Richard Ravitch statement quoted by Michael Barone, "Hold the VAT—taxpayers may prefer spending cuts," *The Examiner*, washingtonexaminer.com, April 25, 2010.

[25] Revision of "Can We Really Afford The Ice Cream?" A story related by an unidentified teacher.

[26] The Rev. William John Henry Boetcker, "Industrial Decalogue", aka, "The American Charter", Committee For Constitutional Government," 1916.

[27] President Gerald R. Ford, Presidential address to a joint session of Congress, August 12, 1974. Ford has also been quoted as having made a similar statement many years earlier, as a representative to the US Congress: "If the government is big enough to give you everything you want, it is big enough to take away everything you have."

[28] Quotation of Winston Churchill, British Prime Minister during the decisive part of World War II.

[29] Statement of George Bernard Shaw, quoted by: Scott J. Hammond, Kevin R. Hardwick, Howard Leslie Lubert, *Classics of American Political and*

Constitutional Thought, Vol. 2:   Reconstruction to the Present, (Indianapolis, Hackett Publishing Company, Inc., 2007), 890.

[30] Presentation by U. S. Senator Jim Inhofe (R-Okla.), Ranking Member of the Senate Environment and Public Works Committee, to expose the cap and trade tax scheme, made on the U. S. Senate Floor, March 8, 2009.

[31] Thomas Jefferson on Politics & Government, writer of the Declaration of Independence and third President of the United States of America.

[32] "Ronald Reagan speaks out on Socialized Medicine", Reagan Foundation - Audio, 1961. (He attributed this to U.S. Socialist Party presidential candidate, Norman Thomas, but it is uncertain if Thomas made that exact statement.)

[33] Alinsky, Saul, *Rules for Radicals: A Pragmatic Primer for Realistic Radicals,* Random House, New York City, 1971.

[34] Drew, John "Meeting Young Obama," *American Thinker,* http://www.americanthinker.com/2011/02/meeting_young_obama.html July 28, 2011, originally dated February 24, 2011.

[35] Op. cit., de Tocqueville.

[36] "Ronald Reagan speaks out on Socialized Medicine", Reagan Foundation - Audio, 1961. (He attributed this to U.S. Socialist Party presidential candidate, Norman Thomas, but it is uncertain if Thomas made that exact statement.)

www.ingramcontent.com/pod-product-compliance
Lightning Source LLC
Chambersburg PA
CBHW060000300526
45794CB00003B/1018